FACING LIFE'S CHALLENGES

FACING BIGOTRY

BY GOLRIZ GOLKAR

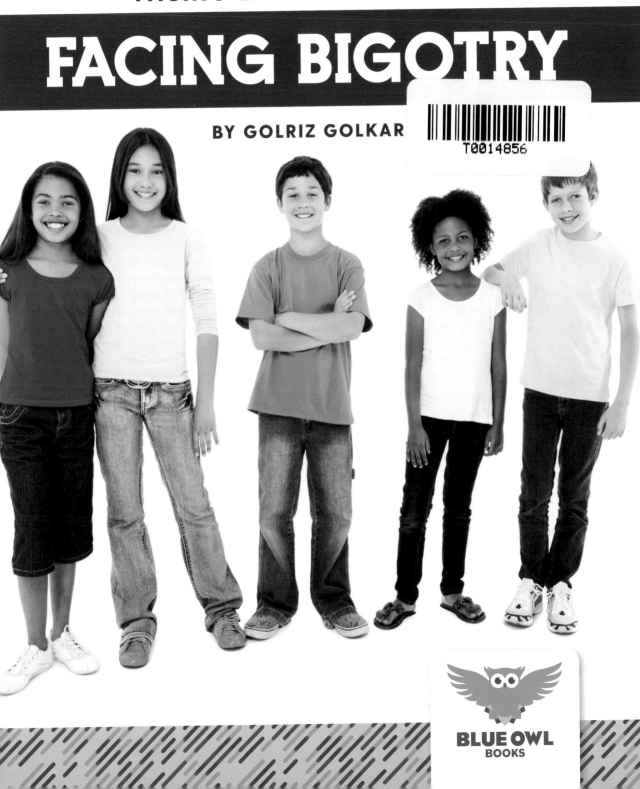

BLUE OWL
BOOKS

TIPS FOR CAREGIVERS

Social and emotional learning (SEL) helps children manage emotions, create and achieve goals, maintain relationships, learn how to feel empathy, and make good decisions. The SEL approach will help children establish positive habits in communication, cooperation, and decision-making. By incorporating SEL in early reading, children will be better equipped to build confidence and foster positive peer networks.

BEFORE READING

Talk to the reader about bigotry. Explain how bigotry can be intolerance of ideas, beliefs, and physical or mental attributes.

Discuss: How do you feel when someone makes fun of something about you? How do you want to respond? Who can help you when someone makes bigoted comments about you or another person?

AFTER READING

Talk to the reader about tolerance. Ask him or her how people can learn to accept and include one another.

Discuss: What steps can you take to be more tolerant of people who are different from you? Can you think of ways to help your friends become more tolerant of others?

SEL GOAL

Students who experience bigotry may struggle to speak up when targeted. They may also have trouble defending others when witnessing bigotry. Help readers find ways to voice their feelings. Divide students into small groups. Encourage them to discuss whether they have ever experienced or witnessed bigotry. How did it make them feel? What did they do to stop it?

TABLE OF CONTENTS

CHAPTER 1

WHAT IS BIGOTRY?

The boys in science club used to tease Ariana. They said girls were not good at science. Ariana proved them wrong. She won first place at the science fair!

Ariana experienced bigotry. Bigotry is **intolerance** of a person or group. People **expressing** it may show **prejudice** against different ideas and beliefs.

Bigotry can **target** a person's **ethnicity**, religion, age, or health. It can also target someone's **race**, **gender**, or **disability**.

You might face bigotry at school or in activities. Strangers might express bigotry. Sometimes, friends and family show bigotry.

TYPES OF BIGOTRY

Sometimes people don't mean to show bigotry. A person may repeat something heard at home. Other times, people are mean on purpose. It is important to know that bigotry is never OK.

Bigotry can make you feel sad, angry, confused, or scared. Never ignore your feelings. Speak up about bigotry. Talk to someone you trust. Everyone deserves to feel like they belong.

CHAPTER 2

WHAT YOU CAN DO

Lynn and Jessie are best friends. Lynn once said Christmas was better than Hanukkah. This made Jessie sad, so she talked to her mom. They invited Lynn to Hanukkah dinner. It helped Lynn realize she was wrong. Hanukkah is special, too!

When you experience bigotry, ask the person why he or she feels that way. Then ask how he or she would feel in your place. If this person is your friend, explain what your friendship means to you. Your friendship will be stronger if you are honest about your feelings.

Jinho's classmates teased him about his name. Others asked if they could call him by an easier name instead. Jinho told them that their comments hurt his feelings. He believes everyone's name is special. His classmates listened to him. Now, they all call him Jinho.

You may get mad when someone says something hurtful. Take a deep breath. Go for a walk. Write your thoughts and feelings in a journal. Talk to someone you trust. Try to remain calm. People will listen better.

WHEN ADULTS SHOW BIGOTRY

Adults can also make bigoted comments. If this happens, you may feel uncomfortable. Ask a parent, teacher, or other trusted adult for help.

journal

CHAPTER 3

HELPING OTHERS

Simon's classmates thought he couldn't play basketball because he uses a wheelchair. Cody included him. Now, Simon plays with everyone else at recess.

If you hear someone making bigoted comments, speak up. Interrupt them. Say, "Stop! Be nice!" If others laugh, never join them. Be an **ally** for the targeted person. Say something kind about him or her.

Someone else may speak up before you do. Join that person. Say, "Yes, I agree!" When many people speak up, bigotry stops.

Speaking up can help others learn **tolerance**. You can also show tolerance by including everyone in group activities.

You can help fight bigotry. Learn about people who seem different from you. Ask them about their **traditions** or language. Listen to others who might be struggling. They may need your friendship.

Tell a trusted adult if anyone makes you feel unsafe or uncomfortable. If we all speak up together, we can help stop bigotry.

SELF-REFLECTION

Think about how you speak to others. If you've said hurtful things, you can change. Think about how you could be a better ally.

GOALS AND TOOLS

GROW WITH GOALS

Bigotry is hard to experience. Try these goals to help you fight bigotry.

Goal: Make a list of different ways people can show bigotry. Write examples of each form of bigotry you listed.

Goal: Think about how bigotry makes you feel. Talk to your family and friends about how bigotry makes them feel.

Goal: Think of ways to include more people in activities. With your friends, make a list of ideas and discuss how each one can help everyone feel included.

TRY THIS!

Bigotry can only stop if people speak up about it. Ask a friend to help you practice what you could say if you witness bigotry.

- Come up with a situation in which someone is showing bigotry. What do they say or do?

- In a calm voice, practice telling the person that you disagree and that he or she should be kinder. You could say, "That's not true," or "That's not fair. Let's be nice."

- Ask your friend to come up with another response to support you. He or she could say, "I also think that's mean. We should stop teasing right now. Let's all do something fun together."

GLOSSARY

ally
A person who joins with another person for a common purpose.

disability
A physical, mental, cognitive, or developmental condition that can limit a person's ability to do certain tasks.

ethnicity
A social group that shares a common culture, religion, or language.

expressing
Showing what you feel or think with words, writing, or actions.

gender
The state of being male or female.

intolerance
Unwillingness to accept actions, customs, beliefs, or opinions that are different from one's own.

prejudice
An opinion or judgment formed unfairly or without knowing all the facts.

race
One of the major groups into which humans can be divided. People of the same race share similar physical characteristics, which are passed from one generation to the next.

target
To select someone or something as an object of attention or attack.

tolerance
Willingness to respect or accept the actions, customs, beliefs, and opinions of others.

traditions
Customs, ideas, or beliefs that are handed down from one generation to the next.

TO LEARN MORE

FACT SURFER

Finding more information is as easy as 1, 2, 3.

1. Go to www.factsurfer.com

2. Enter "**facingbigotry**" into the search box.

3. Choose your book to see a list of websites.

INDEX

Blue Owl Books are published by Jump!, 5357 Penn Avenue South, Minneapolis, MN 55419, www.jumplibrary.com

Library of Congress Cataloging-in-Publication Data

Names: Golkar, Golriz, author.
Title: Facing bigotry / by Golriz Golkar.
Description: Minneapolis, MN: Jump!, Inc., [2023] | Series: Facing life's challenges | Includes index. | Audience: Ages 7–10
Identifiers: LCCN 2021053219 (print)
LCCN 2021053220 (ebook)
ISBN 9781636908076 (hardcover)
ISBN 9781636908083 (paperback)
ISBN 9781636908090 (ebook)
Subjects: LCSH: Discrimination–Juvenile literature. | Prejudices–Juvenile literature. | Toleration–Juvenile literature.
Classification: LCC HM821 .G65 2022 (print)
LCC HM821 (ebook) | DDC 305–dc23/eng/20211101
LC record available at https://lccn.loc.gov/2021053219
LC ebook record available at https://lccn.loc.gov/2021053220

Editor: Eliza Leahy
Designer: Molly Ballanger

Photo Credits: Laboo Studio/Shutterstock, cover (left); Pete Pahham/Shutterstock, cover (right); GlobalStock/iStock, 1; Darrin Henry/Shutterstock, 3; Kues/Shutterstock, 4; fstop123/iStock, 5; Courtney Hale/iStock, 6–7; wavebreakmedia/Shutterstock, 8–9; Shutterstock, 10; Jovica Varga/Shutterstock, 11; FluxFactory/iStock, 12–13 (background); ben bryant/Shutterstock, 12–13 (foreground); Zuraisham Salleh/iStock, 14–15; iStock, 16, 20–21 (foreground); ArtSvetlana/Shutterstock, 17 (background); Juanmonino/iStock, 17 (foreground left); Syda Productions/Shutterstock, 17 (foreground right); New Africa/Shutterstock, 18–19; Artazum/Shutterstock, 20–21 (background).

Printed in the United States of America at Corporate Graphics in North Mankato, Minnesota.